POWER
THE WAVE

A Simplified System to
Build and Manage a Business

PATRICK SMYTH

ENCHANTED
FOREST PRESS
IRVINE, CALIFORNIA

Powering the Wave:
A Simplified System to Build and Manage a Business

www.innovationhabitude.com

Published by Enchanted Forest Press
36 Juneberry
Irvine, CA 92606
www.enchantedforestpress.com

First Publishing July 2010

ISBN 978-0-9828649-0-6

Printed in the United States of America
10 9 8 7 6 5 4 3 2 1

Art Direction, Book Design and Cover Design © 2010
All Rights Reserved by

enchantedforestpress.com

There is a tide in the affairs of men,
Which, taken at the flood, leads on to fortune;
Omitted, all the voyage of their life
Is bound in shallows and in miseries.

—Shakespeare
Julius Caesar

CONTENTS

Thanks to the artists in Montreal.
A picture is worth a thousand words.

INTRODUCTION

Entrepreneurs: people who put everything they have, including themselves, on the line to pursue a dream, to solve a problem in a new way, to change the world, or simply to improve the quality and enjoyment of life. They see risk and rise up to face it with relish. No mountain is too high to climb, and no obstacle too complex to overcome. They operate outside the box of large corporate structures and bureaucratic processes. For many of them, the idea of getting a job is like abandoning everything they believe in. This despite statistics show that nearly ninety percent of new startup businesses fail within two years.

Yet without their creativity, passion, commitment, and steadfast persistence, the waves of change that drive and accelerate innovation and advancement would go dormant. Without their dedication, millions of new jobs and business opportunities would disappear. In many ways, entrepreneurs are the gearbox that drives the engine of progress to sustain our economy and prosperity. Imagine if we could reduce the ninety percent failure rate to just eighty percent. That would double the number of successful new businesses. The result would be an unprecedented engine for growth. I hope that this book will play a small part in achieving that result.

After working with many business leaders at various stages of developing or refocusing their businesses, I noticed a common theme among them. After delivering many seminar presentations to groups of business entrepreneurs, I saw the same pattern of questions arise. The theme I hear repeatedly is, "Just tell me what to do next". It seems that quite a few business leaders and entrepreneurs simply want someone to tell them what the next steps are. If I were in their shoes I would want to start with the big picture-where is my business going and what is the *roadmap* to get there. Then knowing what to do next will have a meaningful context and the next steps may even become self-evident.

This is often the proverbial "can't see the forest for the trees" scenario. Many people focus so intently on the operating details of their business that they cannot take a step back to see the broader context of their business vision and mission. Thousands of entrepreneurs reach this point after attending schools or business conferences to learn the sequence to building and managing a business. The challenge is that there are an infinite number of sequences, each business is unique, and each is in a difference stage of development or maturity.

To complicate matters further, we need to develop multiple elements at the same time and in support of each other. Imagine these steps in the sequence depicted in a linear fashion like a pert chart. The lines linking elements, and the dependencies between them, would create a spaghetti-like pattern. That spaghetti pattern can be very confusing. It will serve to overwhelm people who simply want to know how to proceed—"please, just tell me what to do next!"

Recently, while speaking with a group of entrepreneurs I learned there were several talented and creative people in the audience who had never run a business. I realized that talking about the steps in the business startup process in detail was going to confuse and discourage them. I was also aware that creative people were good at visualizing concepts. I decided that they needed a simplified diagram, or model, showing the steps as elements and their relationship to each other. This graphical model puts the entire business into a simple diagram depicting all aspects of the business to clearly to enhance understanding. By perusing this diagram, what to do next becomes obvious. The relationship between the elements is just as clear. A model so simple that everyone can understand and use it, regardless of their sophistication or experience in managing or leading a business enterprise.

The reality is that multiple things do need attention at the same time, perhaps with differing priorities. Because these items are also interdependent, having a model to use as a leadership control panel can be a very helpful tool. Armed with this tool, I was able to skip attempting to answer the "What's next?" question. Instead, the model and simple diagram I developed helped to establish the big picture context and served as the functional control panel. I presented the model to the group of creative business entrepreneurs at a networking meeting.

After my talk ended, two people came up to me and hugged me. They thanked me for making this process so easy to understand. For the first time they had a clearer appreciation of all of the elements that must be developed and managed to create a successful business venture. I have since presented the model to hundreds of business people and entrepreneurs and the response has been generally the same. I refer to this diagram as the gearbox of a business venture.

As you will see in the diagram (Figure 1) below, three gears need to align and synchronize in order for a business enterprise to achieve its goals. A gap or weakness in one gear will ripple through the whole system. I focus my client advisory work on the Business layer since it serves at the intersection between the business leader, and the tools required to execute the business vision successfully. My goal is to simplify the navigation of the journey of analyzing, planning, and building successful business ventures.

The model works regardless of whether you are a brand new startup, or a mature business looking for a more effective executive management tool. This model comprises three primary gears, or layers, each supported by three key elements. It all starts in the middle of the gear labeled YOU. As you will see, what happens on the outside of the diagram is just as dependent on the starting point—YOU.

This book lays out the rationale for, and builds the model, focusing on one element per chapter. In the end you will gain a deeper and yet more comprehensive understanding of the gearbox that drives a business enterprise. This improves your ability to lead and grow your business and to recognize easily what elements need adjustment or development to make your venture successful. Armed with the gearbox, you will become the power behind the next wave of change.

YOUR BUSINESS GEARBOX

People tend to remember things better in groups of three. The "gearbox" model conveniently comprises three layers (or gears), each consisting of three elements. This makes the diagram and model easy to remember and easy to relate to without additional prompting or input. Each layer is itself a system and all three layers are interdependent. As we will see, an issue with one element of one of the layers can affect all of the other layers, and thereby significantly affect the ability of the business to succeed.

The design of this book follows and effectively builds this model. Three sections each comprise three chapters examining each element of the model in detail. In addition to clarifying the role of each element, I have highlighted the relationship and dependencies between the elements and layers. The model is a system, and each layer is a system within the model. The result is that whatever the stage of your business right now, you will develop a clearer and simpler model that enables you to manage the entire system as a whole. You will be able to navigate a path forward with greater clarity of purpose and with a new awareness of the complete picture of the business in which you operate.

The three core layers, or layers, of this model are labeled as follows: 1. YOU; 2. Business; and 3. Execution.

The first layer, YOU, determines your potential to be effective, almost regardless of the business or vocation you choose. With a positive attitude, a clear purpose, and the knowledge needed to accomplish that purpose, you are potent.

The second layer, Business, determines the core elements on which a successful business concept can be built. Businesses begin and end with their vision, or purpose, combined with the strategy to accomplish that vision, and supported by the leadership to make it all happen.

The third layer, Execution, describes the tools and resources you will need to execute the business. This includes intellectual and financial capital, the systems required to execute the strategy, and the people to run the business and support your customers. For any business to maximize productivity, all elements of all three layers must align to work together.

With these three layers defined and well synchronized, your business gearbox is capable of driving your business forward effectively. As defined, this geabox can only provide internal information on how well the business may be executing. To complete the model, we need to add fuel to the engine. This fuel is the cash paid to you by customers for your products and services. Without customers, you have no business, so we need to add another layer. In addition to customers, two other elements will add oil and grease to the gearbox to enable it to function more efficiently. They are suppliers and partners.

Without customers, you have no business

This final layer facilitates the measurement or the effectiveness of our business model and operation. In fact, to make most effective use of the model, the starting point should be the customers in this outer layer. Then work your way in to the middle. You may find that work needs to be done near the center of the model. Knowing what customers and other outer layers need will establish the appropriate context to assure optimal alignment throughout the business. We discuss this measurement layer in the chapter called "Measuring Performance" toward the end of this book.

> Method goes far to prevent trouble in business: for it makes the task easy, hinders confusion, saves abundance of time, and instructs those that have business depending, both what to do and what to hope.
>
> —William Penn

The beauty of this model is that the sequencing of where to start and what to do next is obvious by looking at the diagram. Likewise, focusing on any element allows you to see what else it affects across the business. Whether developing a new business or leading and evolving an existing business, examining your business against this model on a regular basis will keep you focused on the right big picture. Knowing where all the trees are in the forest and why they are there helps you manage the whole forest. You can then spend more time serving your customers and less time fighting internal fires.

Section I:
YOU ARE YOUR BUSINESS

CHAPTER 1:

Introducing the YOU Gear

At the center of any endeavor is a leader, creator, or inventor. Everything else that happens in the business is directly impacted by the effectiveness of this person—or as our model indicates—YOU. Three key elements need to be clarified and aligned in order for you to function to your potential: your attitude, your purpose, and the knowledge needed to accomplish your purpose. This is true regardless of your aspirations in business or otherwise.

As you will see throughout this discussion–everything begins with attitude. Without a positive, constructive attitude, you will struggle to accomplish almost anything. Self-limiting beliefs, or fears, beset most people and these issues play a huge role in defining our attitudes. They also directly influence the decisions we make. Even if you are clear about your purpose, these attitude challenges can stop you from achieving it.

Everything begins with attitude

Next, you will need to clarify your purpose. I am specifically talking here about your personal purpose, not the purpose for your business–that will come later. It is very important that you know what inspires you, and to learn to find people, products, and services that would benefit by that motivation.

Finally, in order to effectively do anything about your purpose, you will need to acquire relevant knowledge to convert your purpose into action. With these three ingredients in place, you will reach a level of potency as an individual. This newfound potential may have many different applications. For now, we are going to focus your potential on a business concept.

CHAPTER 2:
Attitude

Almost every human endeavor begins and ends with attitude. Regardless of the success or failure of any venture, or the pursuit of any new dream, attitude most often determines the outcome. The interesting dimension, unlike so many obstacles that we may face in life, is that attitude is simply a matter of choice. You cannot decide the weather, the price of gasoline, or a myriad of other factors that may significantly affect your progress. You can decide your attitude. You choose how you respond to obstacles, real or imagined, or to perceived difficult people who you need in order to help you succeed. Your attitude is the one key determinant that will allow you to rise above all of those things. The one thing you can control every time is your attitude.

I believe the single most significant decision I can make on a day-to-day basis is my choice of attitude. It is more important than my past, my education, my bankroll, my successes or failures, fame or pain, what other people think of me or say about my circumstances, my position, or me. Attitude keeps me going or cripples my progress.

It alone fuels my fire or assaults my hope. When my attitudes are right, there is no barrier too high, no valley too deep, no dream too extreme, and no challenge too great for me.

—Charles Swindoll

Understanding the impact of your choice of attitude will make the difference in determining your perseverance and resilience to lead your business successfully to achieve your goals. It will determine your ability to maintain a positive outlook and inspire others in difficult times. If self-limiting beliefs or personal fears weigh you down, then you will have difficulty choosing a positive attitude and even more difficulty influencing others positively.

Think about who might be included in the list of "others". Included are employees, management, investors, partners, suppliers, and customers (the ultimate payers of your bills). Without the ability to influence these people positively, a business leader cannot possibly hope to succeed. Choosing a positive attitude is the first mandatory step and it is a choice to make every day. Many new challenges will emerge—how will you choose to meet them?

> Choosing a positive attitude is the first mandatory step

Occasionally entrepreneurs ask me to review business plans and detailed financial projections to see if I can help to improve their ability to raise capital. After a brief conversation about their capital raising efforts, a clearer picture about their predicament emerges. The trouble is not with their numbers or other assertions in their documents. The problem is with their attitude. That realization sometimes leads to a different type of coaching session or process to remove the fears and other mental blockages and convert the person into a confident leader. Depending on the person's willingness to recognize and adjust their attitude, this works very well with some, and for others, it can be a big waste of time.

Can everyone or anyone be a leader? That may indeed be possible. First, they must WANT to do it, then they must COMMIT to do it, and then they must simply just DO it. Thousands of people appear to be addicted to motivational speakers and conferences. They also attend business conferences, listen to endless successful business speakers, and still they accomplish nothing. Too many of them confuse the euphoria of feeling good after attending such a seminar with motivation. Feeling good is not motivation. Motivation also does not come from someone else. Motivation implies that you are inspired to take action toward something specific. If you attend countless seminars and still do nothing, you are not motivated.

The biggest antidote to fear is action

The biggest antidote to fear is action. Once you take an action, even if it seems quite small in the face of the overall challenge, you will have accomplished something. Do that again a few times and pretty soon you have accomplished quite a bit. Then you will see that action is the clearest indicator of performance and motivation.

Howard Schultz likes to tell the story about the time when he was struggling to turn his small coffee shop business into a unique and successful enterprise. Faced with a seemingly desperate financial situation, his father-in-law sat him down on a park bench and asked him to give up his "dream and hobby" and to get a "real job" to support his family. But Mr. Schultz could not let go of his dream. He knew, deep down, that his idea would work. More determined than ever, he went on to build the most successful coffee shop business the world has known. Most likely, there is a Starbucks store near you.

New ideas pass through three periods:
1) It can't be done;
2) It probably can be done, but it's not worth doing;
3) I knew it was a good idea all along.

Sound familiar? What happens when you get that great idea and you know, in your heart of hearts, it has the potential to be the breakthrough for which you have been searching?

First, you are excited and you have to share it with somebody. The best place to start is your friends and family. Naturally, they will share your enthusiasm, and maybe even help you to get started, right? WRONG! Family members are great for adding one more phase to the beginning of Mr. Clarke's process, and that is, "You can't do it". Yes, you. Why do they do this?

Sometimes family members feel a need to protect you from "yourself–or so they think. Your great idea can be hard for them to grasp at first. Your idea may be very ambitious compared to anything they know about you, or themselves. They would prefer that you stay in the safety of the little box you are in right now. That way, nobody gets hurt or embarrassed, starting with themselves, by association, with your crazy idea.

Assume, after your first wave of frustration with your family, that you remain committed to the idea. You then reach out to business associates, advisors, and other "experts" in the field. Surely they will see the light and be more independently objective than your family. Maybe. Do not be surprised by awkward responses as people don't quite understand or appreciate the merits of your idea.

> Every really new idea looks crazy at first.
>
> —Alfred North Whitehead

Yes, get ready to hear, "It can't be done". Or, how about, "It's been done before", or, "It's been tried before and failed, and therefore it will fail again" Aargh!! What is driving those responses? For many it is simply fear. For others, the idea may be beyond their ability to imagine. Does that make it a bad idea? Absolutely, it does not.

Occasionally, they will act as though they are trying to help you avoid risk by challenging your ability to bring the idea to life. They may say things like, "If 'big bad companies' steal your idea, then what will you do?". They will undoubtedly throw up many smoke screens to veil their own uncertainty and fears at not wanting to stick their necks out for something so risky.

> Don't worry about people stealing an idea. If it's original, you will have to ram it down their throats.
>
> —Howard Aiken

Somewhere along the way in the journey of your idea, you will find people who are willing to validate the inspiration. This could be in the form of scientific research, or letters of intent to buy your new product, or recommendations from experts in the field. Now your idea has credibility! Or so you believe. Do not think for a minute that you will persuade the cynics with this new found wisdom, insight, and independent authority.

That brings you to the next step in the idea process, "It probably can be done, but it's not worth doing." Their own fear of failure and their natural tendency toward risk avoidance is so strong they will not allow themselves to see the potential. So they raise the bar by asking you to justify the value of the idea, assuming it was accomplished.

Real cynics or skeptics will keep throwing new hurdles at you no matter how many times you satisfy their objections.

> The soft-minded man always fears change. He feels security in the status quo, and he has an almost morbid fear of the new. For him, the greatest pain is the pain of a new idea.
>
> —Martin Luther King

You must remain committed to the belief that potential investors, partners, buyers, and supporters will, over time, come around to your idea. When you finally break through, do not be surprised by the change in tone of all those friends, family members, and other cynics.

They were so sure that you and your idea were heading for certain disaster. Now they are suddenly becoming the geniuses who were responsible for your success. They then create the last phase of the idea process, "I knew it was a good idea all along". Or, how about, "I knew he could do it all along", or, "Heck, I was the one who told him to keep going when he wanted to give it all up", or, "You know, I remember the day we came up with the idea on my front porch".

Do not be annoyed or frustrated with them. Instead, give them all as much credit as they want. Thank them for their encouragement. They will revel in the recognition and your idea will gain more support. Better yet, they will respect you even more for it.

Every new idea faces these obstacles. People resist change, they fear the unknown, and they are comfortable in their safe little boxes. It takes a special commitment and dedication to an idea to push doggedly through all the dissension that you will face as you explore your idea. Sound business ideas that have real potential can have many of the risks addressed by creating a solid vision and strategic plan, and aligning yourself with key people who will become powerful champions of your dream. The ultimate driver, however, has to be YOU.

> Get a good idea and stay with it. Dog it, and work at it until it's done right.
>
> —Walt Disney

CHAPTER 3:

Purpose

I met an interesting man during a break at a business conference. He had earned two Ph.D. degrees in Mathematics and Engineering from an Ivy League University. As he introduced himself, he uttered these words, "I'm stuck and I think you can help me." Since we were at a business conference, I thought he was talking about a business issue. Instead, he said he felt something was pulling him in an entirely new direction. He was struggling with his own inner fears and beliefs. If I chose to respond to his request, I would be faced with an amazing test. It was puzzling to me that he had decided to share openly a personal conflict with a complete stranger. It struck me that in spite of his incredible education and obvious intellect, he felt trapped.

For a moment, I wondered whether I could even help this man. This was not a typical conversation for me—as I usually focus on business issues and stay away from the personal side. I concluded that if a man of this caliber placed such confidence in me then I had a responsibility to accept the assignment. I asked him a few questions to learn a little more about his situation. I was able to guide him through a process that enabled him to clarify the issues he was facing. I outlined a process for converting his beliefs and fears into actionable decisions. Forty minutes after we met, he left the meeting saying "Wow that was very powerful". He was now equipped with a tool that could help him to make the transition from scientist and educator to entrepreneur and business owner.

Over the next few months, several people approached me in business settings with almost exactly the same request. That is, "I'm stuck and I think you can help me". One of these was a young woman who had a dream and a passion for a new project that would take her far away from her experience and education to date. She was so moved by my conversation with her that she immediately shared her dream with a business executive at the conference. Amazingly, that man was running a project that needed someone who was passionate about exactly the thing that interested this young woman. He asked her to join his team. That is what can happen when you align yourself with your passion.

Later that evening, the same young woman dragged a man by his shirtsleeves over to come and see me. She said, "That thing you did for me this morning, you need to do that for him". Of course, I was happy to talk to him about whatever caused him to be stuck. He told me that his fear was about money. He had never had money in his family from his childhood days, and he was concerned that if he received any money he would somehow cause it to be lost. The problem for this man was that he was about to meet a prospective investor for his business. He was almost panicking. About an hour later, he left with a better understanding of how to rationalize and make productive decisions about his fears. I also showed him a technique to overcome his fear in real time-just as he would experience it before walking into the room with the investor.

The next day I saw him walking through the hotel lobby. I caught his attention and asked him how the meeting went. He first apologized for not having enough time to do everything I had shared with him. However, he said he must have done enough of it correctly because the investor decided to make the investment. He told me that it was all due to my support and coaching to him. That would have been enough to make my day. He then went on to say that when he received the money from the investor, he would like to make a substantial investment in my company. What?! I had not even thought about raising investment funding for my company, so naturally his response floored me.

I have received quite a few email messages from people I have helped to refocus. These messages convinced me that there was something important happening there and I needed to pay attention to it. The question was how to honor the requests for help and not let free coaching overwhelm my business. The answer came from the people themselves. Some of the email messages encouraged me to create a program so that I could help a lot more people. One even wrote that I would have their unconditional support if I were to do so. Some have since become customers who trust me to guide them through the development of business visions and strategic plans to grow or launch their businesses. Others encouraged me to write a book on this process so that I can reach even more people and in much greater depth.

I have since conducted several workshops in multiple cities. A friend of mine came to a workshop with an uncooperative attitude. Basically, he thought he was doing me a favor simply by sitting in the room, just so he could say he did. He was in for a surprise. About a third of the way through the workshop he suddenly spoke out, "I just had a revelation!" The process, in spite of his resistance, revealed a pattern of compromises in his life. He though he knew who he was. He now understood that he had made a series of compromises driven by fear over many years. He saw that he could indeed choose a new way forward. In his workbook, he wrote in big bold letters, "I WANT TO BE KING!"

For an athlete to function properly, he must be intent. There has to be a definite purpose and goal if you are to progress. If you are not intent about what you are doing, you aren't able to resist the temptation to do something else that might be more fun at the moment.

John Wooden

A college professor invited me to conduct the workshop for his graduate business students at the start of their fall semester. I was happy to do it, as this was a new audience in a new type of venue. He saw it as an opportunity to help his students to open their minds and realize their potential. Then whatever he taught them would have a greater chance of being applied. A couple of the students invited me to meet their employers so that I could help more people at their place of business. The professor also participated in the workshop with his students. After the students had left the classroom, he came to me and shared that this process had clarified an issue that had plagued him since childhood. For the first time he was able to put words to it and clearly understand and articulate the issue. Now at the age of sixty, he would finally be able to let the issue go. How do you put a price on that?

A good friend of mine once told me "You don't suffer fools lightly". I thought it was a compliment at the time. I never really understood the concept of patience. I was very confident in my ability to get things done. I would focus my attention on assertive people who demonstrated that they would act fast. Unfortunately, sometimes I overlooked people around me who may have had a lot to contribute. These recent experiences helping others in their businesses, with their dreams, and overcoming their own fears and self-limiting beliefs have changed all that. Knowing that I can help to empower people to become effective leaders in business and in life is a humbling notion. It is they, after all, who need to grow and execute their businesses. That requires that I respect their strengths and help them develop their potential.

More importantly, it required that I learned to put the needs of the other person in front of my own. It came by learning to listen to them and by asking questions. Open, non-judgmental questions communicate clearly two things: first, my primary concern is to learn so that I can help them move forward productively; and second, I care about their interests and needs and value their insights in helping to guide them. When you ask open questions about their needs, people will believe that you care about them. They will respond by trusting you to lead them because they believe you will consider their needs along the way.

Leaders who cooperate by listening and focusing on the needs of others before their own are likely to realize significantly greater performance. That is true for the leaders themselves and the organizations they lead as well. This approach strengthens the relationship between the team and the leader and strengthens their commitment to produce. In the long term, this develops a strong and loyal following of people who will gladly, and openly, recommend you to others. This trust and respect creates a phenomenally powerful growth engine that is practically unstoppable and costs very little.

CHAPTER 4:
Knowledge

Once you have clarity about your purpose–that is, your personal purpose for your life–you need to acquire knowledge about this purpose in order for you to have any potential at all to accomplish it. Lack of knowledge about a purpose will breed fear as you face the unknown, not confident that you can accomplish anything. This fear could completely prevent you from ever taking any action for your purpose. This creates stress, internal conflict, lack of self-esteem and confidence, and can disrupt your life.

You may even accept that you will never accomplish your purpose and push it aside so that you can continue down the path you are already following. That just prolongs the internal conflict and sets you up for a major disappointment. Do you really want to look back on your life and say "If only I...." when you knew that all you had to do was learn a little about your purpose so you could execute it? Lack of knowledge may also breed ineptness as you attempt to execute your purpose but stumble around blindly. Then you become despondent and yo may even turn off other team members who are depending on you.

> To succeed in business, to reach the top, an individual must know all it is possible to know about that business.
>
> —J. Paul Getty

The answer to this issue is "knowledge". With knowledge, you have the ability to make informed decisions. You have the ability to decide and then act on those decisions. Knowledge eliminates the "What if...?" questions we ask ourselves when we do not have intelligent questions that would equip us with information to make a decision. Each "What if...?" question is a statement about something negative that may happen. There is no answer to the question and no information is supplied or even implied.

> Knowledge eliminates the "What if...?" questions

Instead of asking "What if...", we should be asking questions that would help us to acquire knowledge to eliminate the unknowns. To provide clues about the actions and directions we should be taking. Each time you act, you are making progress. With each step of progress, your accomplishments grow. So does your confidence, motivation, and your knowledge of what it takes to make your purpose successful. Each small step moves you closer to your target and pretty soon you will start to redefine your own self worth and awareness in the context of your purpose.

How about knowledge in business? I worked with an entrepreneur who actually told me she did not need to know everything that was going on in her business. She would say, "I don't need to know everything because I'm the CEO—I get other people to do the work". Yes, I did say she was an entrepreneur. She had an interesting idea with the potential to make significant difference in the development of millions of children.

She was assembling a team of people who would help her develop her product, to secure investment funding and to develop her go to market strategy and all of the other core elements needed to execute the business. She expected that she could simply assemble the team and then drive them to develop and deliver the business for her. She had apparently never heard the term "sweat equity".

Founders of companies earn the large percentage of ownership in large measure by the dedicated and relentless effort that they apply to their success.

It is true that a good CEO surrounds themselves with outstanding team leaders who can lead and execute core elements of the business strategy. However, the CEO must lead the company inside and out–with employees, management, shareholders, investors, partners, suppliers, and ultimately with customers. The CEO must know exactly how the vision and mission of the company translates into products, services, operations, branding, employee culture, financial performance, and relationships with partners and suppliers. The CEO may not know the specific details of how every task is accomplished. He or she will most definitely want to know why the tasks are undertaken, what the relationship is between them, and how they support the accomplishment of the company's strategy. The CEO delegates the work, not the strategic direction and bottom line performance of the business.

POTENTIAL:

At this stage in building up the gears of your business venture, if you have aligned your attitude, your purpose and the knowledge required to execute it, you have reached a point of personal potency. You have the attitude and will to do it, you know what you want to do, and you have the knowledge to begin taking the steps to accomplish it. Whatever direction you choose to take your purpose, you now have the potential to make it successful. You will see later on how important these attributes are to your overall venture.

SECTION II:
THE BUSINESS CONCEPT

CHAPTER 5:

Introducing the Business Concept

To establish an effective foundation for your business, we find, once again, three key elements. The first and most important is the vision, or purpose, of your business. Everything else you do you must anchor to and be designed to support the accomplishment of this vision. The vision is the outcome you are proposing to create for your customers in the future. Remember in Section I we discussed your personal purpose in the section about YOU?

If your personal purpose aligns with your business vision (or purpose), you will have a significantly higher likelihood of success. They do not have to be exactly the same, but they must support each other. The most powerful motivator comes from accomplishing something that aligns with your purpose. You may be successful in your business in financial terms if these purposes do not align. However, you will never be happy, and there will come a time when that conflict will cause a disruption.

Align personal purpose with business vision

The next element is the strategy for your business. This is where all the detailed hard work goes into answering the question of how you intend to execute your vision. This includes:

- what problem you are solving

- the solutions you will provide
- the benefits of that solution to your customers
- how big the market opportunity is
- the competition and why you are better
- what your marketing approach will be
- who will be your partners and alliances and suppliers
- how you will develop and manufacture your products and services
- and ultimately your financial projections showing exactly how much profit this business will produce over time.

Again, all of this work must focus on achieving your vision. This requires quite a bit of knowledge and once again, you can see the connection with your personal purpose. If you are passionate about acquiring knowledge for your personal purpose, and that aligns with your business vision, then you will develop a compelling business strategy.

Finally, in order to make anything happen in this business you need leadership. That begins with you. If your attitude is not productive, what kind of leader will you be? Of course, leadership in business includes the other members of your team, all of whom must be positively motivated and committed to your vision. At this level, you have a solid foundation for a business concept. To execute the business requires the third gear. Like a racecar coming off the manufacturing floor, it has awesome potential but it needs fuel to make it go.

CHAPTER 6:
Vision

Many small businesses run by the seat of the pants of the founder/owners. The fortunate ones have created a product or service, sold it to a few people, and decided they are successful. Therefore, they will just keep doing what they are already doing because it apparently works. Then what happens when things go wrong? I met just such a man who had developed a great product and he had successfully sold it to a very large client, who accounted for about ninety percent of his sales volume. He was rightfully pleased with the rapid growth in sales after landing this company as a client.

Unfortunately, his success gained the attention of a very large industrial supplier. They were concerned that his continued success with this and with other large clients would affect their business significantly. They paid a visit to the client and made them an offer that combined pricing, product breadth and services. This small business simply could not match the offer. When the decision came, ninety percent of his business dried up instantly. He had no contingency plan and was not prepared to overcome this loss.

The CEO of this small business lacked a vision for his company. He simply sold to anyone who would buy and when a large client came along he dedicated all of his effort to serving that one customer. Had he developed a clear vision and strategic plan for his business, he would have ensured that he continued to develop and invest in other customer segments and use the one large client to help pay for his growth. The vision drives the bigger picture and helps to assure that your efforts remain focused and balanced in achieving it.

> Vision—It reaches beyond the thing that is, into the conception of what can be. Imagination gives you the picture. Vision gives you the impulse to make the picture your own.
>
> —Robert Collier

Vision sets the compass direction and allows everything you do to align to move in that direction. A very astute person said that if you do not know where you are going you are guaranteed to end up wherever you are. But where will that be exactly? In the story of Alice in Wonderland, Alice arrived at a fork in the road and asked the Cheshire cat which way she should go. The cat replied with a question, "Where do you want to end up?" Alice replied that she did not know, and the cat wisely added, "Then it does not matter which road you choose." Of course, in life and in business a physical destination it is not necessarily what we seek. Rather we need a clear vision of our purpose. What are we proposing to achieve and what outcomes do we want to produce?

Vision sets the compass

We all recognize the CEO who does not seem to be able to make a decision. Every decision appears to go into a black hole, or worse-into analysis by a committee! How about the creative entrepreneur who seems to think they can launch five different business ideas at the same time? Then there is the IT Department that is in permanent crisis mode putting out fires one after the other. What about the VP of Marketing that cannot seem to explain what he accomplished by spending all that money? Many creative people challenge themselves by taking on too many projects at the same time with no particular sense of priority.

Sometimes people wander aimlessly from one project to another without making any significant progress in any of them—the grass is always greener on the other side. Aesop told the fable of the ant and the grasshopper: The grasshopper spent all summer singing, while the ant was busy storing food. The grasshopper jumped from one green leaf to the next, devouring his way through the summer, without a care in the world, and without any thought as to what came next. Then winter came, and everyone knows how the fable ends. If you have no focus or purpose to the work you do, you can be sure to end up in a place you don't want to be-or even out of business altogether.

Other people will focus on minute details to keep themselves busy and to appear to be doing something productive. That is rather like reorganizing your sock drawer in an earthquake. In business, these behaviors and lack of focus can be disastrous. At the strategic level, business focus comes from establishing a clear long-term vision and mission for your business. Then all of your plans and activities can align with the goal of achieving that mission. There will always be distractions and new opportunities and challenges that come along during the journey. By anchoring yourself to your mission, you will greatly enhance your potential to be successful.

If you are an existing business struggling for clarity, where else could you look to for help in focusing yourself? A really good starting point to look for inspiration is your customers. Ask them why they buy from you. Ask them if they are delighted with your product or service. If not, why not? If yes, then why? Both answers lead you to a place of focusing on correcting something in order to do it better. Alternatively, it could mean focusing on what you are already doing well and doing more of it for more customers. If you are a new startup venture and don't have any customers yet, go out and ask people who would be good target buyers of your product. Ask them what they think about the idea and if they would purchase it. If not, why not? If yes, then why?

Perhaps you find that things seem to be going rather well with your customers, but you are still not gaining the clarity of focus you need. Then you need a new approach. An excellent next place to look is at your biggest competitors. What do they do well, and why? What do they not do well, and why? The answer to those questions might tell you about where you need to focus. Compare the information gathered to what your customer told you. This may yield new issues that you need to deal with based on competitor actions.

Maybe you can preempt them and take advantage of the situation, or else they are most likely going to make your life difficult. Having a clear focused direction can play a big role in causing competitors to react to you rather than forcing you to react to them.

> Nothing focuses the mind better than the constant sight of a competitor who wants to wipe you off the map.
>
> —Wayne Calloway, CEO of PepsiCo

Doing a little bit of many different things can keep you very busy, but that can be at the expense of real progress. You must choose a direction—ideally focused on your vision-in order to make any progress at all. Otherwise, you will be like Alice, wandering aimlessly, and not going anywhere in particular, yet guaranteed that you will end up wherever you are.

Why do so many new business ventures start with such enthusiasm for a new idea, only to stop dead in their tracks a short while later? It may be convenient to assume the product or service is simply not a good match for the market. That assumption would most likely prove to be just plain wrong.

You had a great idea for a new product or service and you started selling it to anyone you could find that would buy. Your business took off and one by one, you picked up a decent customer list. You thought you were successful in chasing your dream. Then after a couple of years, you find yourself stalled. After all this time, you seem to have hit a wall.

No matter how hard you work, you cannot seem to break through. How do you make this business grow? What happened? Many new business owners reach this stalled position believing they need to control every aspect of every activity in their company. Over-controlling everything severely restricts any sense of empowerment from the team whom they depend on to execute.

Start with your attitude and the habits you adopt along the way. Adjust your attitude to separate you from your business vision, or dream. You [personally] are not your dream. Although your purpose and your business purpose need to be aligned, when raising capital you are selling an opportunity to invest in the business. You are an important shepherd or steward of your business vision. You can then develop a more objective and balanced perspective on the real potential for your business. That will help you assess the resources and expertise you need to make it happen.

If you keep tying yourself to the dream, you will constantly create limitations on what you are willing, or believe you are able, to do to pursue the dream. You will probably over-control it and constrain it from growing. Worse yet, the vision may overwhelm you as it expands in scope and size.

PUTTING YOUR VISION INTO WORDS

Develop a clear and objective vision for your business before you begin the strategic planning process. This work is essential and perhaps the most important work that you, as leader of the business, can do. With a clear vision, or statement about the future you want your business to create, you can confidently begin planning. Establish long-term goals. Gain the commitment of key people inside and outside of your business. Plan the activities, deliverables, and milestones needed to accomplish the plan. Estimate the revenues, costs, resources, time, and capital needed to accomplish your vision.

> Good business leaders create a vision, articulate the vision, passionately own the vision, and relentlessly drive it to completion.
> —Jack Welch, former chief executive of General Electric Corp

The planning process includes short-term plans for the next 90 to 120 days that lead progress toward the long term. Having a clear vision allows each of these initiatives and the people you depend on to develop and execute plans appropriately aligned with a common purpose. Following these steps will dramatically reduce the complexity of your vision and clarifies for you how to accomplish it. Better yet, it greatly increases the potential for you to achieve success.

Use the mantra, "big plans; little steps" as a constant reminder of the need to stay focused and committed to your vision. At the same time, stay equally focused and committed to the planning process required to achieve it. Redo your vision and strategic planning process each year. Constantly adjust your business as market and competitive forces change. You and your team will be able to make sure every little step takes you just a little closer to the reality of your vision.

Big plans, little steps

You may succeed at directing and delegating the work required to accomplish your vision. However, the real key to successful execution comes from the words Jack Welch used, "... passionately own the vision, and relentlessly drive it to completion." Your employees and other team members will assess and frequently emulate your behavior, regardless of what you say.

Clearly communicate your vision for your company frequently and as directly as possible to all team members. They will only commit to your vision and pursue it with a passion of their own if they see this passion and commitment in you first. Do not delegate this assignment and do not underestimate its importance. Take the big plans; little steps approach, and stay relentlessly focused on controlling the focus on your vision. Then you and your entire team can drive your vision to successful completion.

Consider this: what if your personal purpose (from Section I), does not align with the vision (or business purpose) of your company? At some point there is a train wreck coming. You may measure yourself as successful in financial or other numeric terms for a while. Eventually, the internal conflict between your own purpose and that of your business will surface and disrupt your life. You will be frustrated and bored with "work" and look to make a change. Why? Because your internal purpose is very personal and needs to be satisfied by direct personal interaction between you and the way the purpose may manifest itself.

Take a simple example: let's say you acquired a factory that makes better mousetraps. People are buying this better mousetrap in droves because it is just that good. For a while you are excited and growing wealthier each day as products fly out of the factory. Every day, you spend a lot of time on the factory floor making sure the operation is running smoothly. But what if your internal purpose had something to do with helping people to acquire leadership skills or teaching children life skills so they can enter the world as young adults more productively? At some point, you will become frustrated with your time on the factory floor because it does not address the basic needs of your own core purpose. Additionally, you will not be successful at motivating others to achieve success with a purpose when it is plain for all to see that you have no passion.

CHAPTER 7:

Strategy

Literally hundreds of entrepreneurs have said to me "Just tell me what to do next". Now consider building your business that way. Imagine building a staircase with one hundred steps. The foundation for each and every step must be in place in order to support the steps as you go upwards. Clearly as you build a solid foundation, you will find that adding and climbing the subsequent steps becomes easier. Once the foundation is in place, your focus can easily shift to adding and climbing the remaining steps as fast as you can. After reaching the third step, you seem to have the hang of this process. You can now look forward and see exactly how to build the remainder of the steps. For the first time, you have a clear vision of the end game, and you can actually see how you are going to get there. Your confidence and enthusiasm have never been higher.

> Strategy is a style of thinking, a conscious and deliberate process, an intensive implementation system, the science of insuring future success.
>
> —Pete Johnson

At this point, you have two choices to make. The wise choice would be to continue building the foundation and steps exactly as you now see them. Your experiences, combined with the clarity you have gained about the path to the top, have positioned you well for success. Alternatively, you could let your enthusiasm turn into impatience and go for the shortcut. You can decide it is time for the helicopter plan. You let all of your prior judgment and planning fly out the window. Surprisingly, many leaders do this despite learning by experience that creating a strong foundation enables the building of the steps, starting with the first step. Since you can see them so clearly, you decide to jump to step forty-two.

The helicopter flies high enough so you can drop a tall pole that is the correct height for step forty-two. Then you climb out on to it and celebrate the achievement. You are a hero! You have left all of those other suckers behind by leaping forward while they slowly and doggedly build their plans. Then you turn your focus forward to step forty-three. Suddenly, the gap between forty-two and forty-three is a chasm. There is no foundation supporting forty-three and guess what? There is no place for that helicopter to land to pick you up and try that pole trick again. Worse yet, you have discovered that the world has become a rather wobbly place. Balancing that tall thin pole to keep it vertical to support you and your team and all the promises you have made to the marketplace is becoming a mighty challenge.

> Champions know there are no shortcuts to the top. They climb
> the mountain one-step at a time. They have no use for helicopters!
> —Judi Adler

If a helicopter pilot and a mountain climber both reached the same summit, which one has a greater achievement? Which of the two has truly understood and overcome the challenges of the mountain? That foundation of knowledge and experience under step forty-two is a weak and flimsy pole. It certainly cannot support adding more steps for you to proceed with your journey. Now you are stuck. You realize that in order to go forward you have to go back and build the foundation that was required in steps four through forty-one. To add to the challenge, you have to keep step forty-two afloat and balance precariously while you go back and work on the earlier steps in the right order. Do you have sufficient resource and capacity to take all of this on, or will the effort cause you to falter permanently.

Assume you even make it back to step forty-two with a new solid foundation behind you, you may find that you have to rebuild step forty-two completely as well. This is because it was not built on the proper foundation. In order for it to play its proper role in helping you get to your goal-step one hundred—you will need to rebuild it. Meanwhile you have customers, employees, investors, and a lot of other resources and expectations invested in what the original step forty-two was promising. Getting all of that back on track with your new ("original") foundational steps is another challenge and resource drain.

What does the helicopter plan produce?

1. Significant disruption and diversion to an otherwise clear plan.

2. A major drain on resources. You must first go back, rebuild the foundation, and then the earlier steps while keeping the new step going in some fashion.

3. Significant confusion. You must rebuild step forty-two while managing to reset the expectations created by it.

You always have to come back and work on the steps you missed. It takes twice the energy to do this, and it is very inefficient. Along the way, you will find that many of the steps you thought you had completed you now have to redo. By finally following the correct sequence of steps, you have built a new foundation and better platform on which to move to the next step. Old "completed" steps may have been built on shaky ground and now need reworking. This rework causes you to spend time and energy that takes you away from making progress on the next step. The combination of rework and parallel working on steps at different stages in the process can be sufficient impedance to choke your project to a dead stop. Imagine if you had devoted all that resource and time to the original plan.

The old adage, "less haste, more speed" seems apt advice to people who make that fateful helicopter plan choice. Large complex projects including business startups, new ventures, product launches, and corporate branding initiatives can all benefit greatly from leadership that understands and commits to the idea that you need to slow down before you can accelerate. By diligently following the plan you so carefully developed and is proved to be working, you will be in a better position to go faster later on when it really counts. The kind of speed that powers the momentum to drive your business to success comes from a solid foundation built on planning, research, testing, practice, and leadership commitment to stay with the program.

Slow down in order to accelerate

"But what about change?" you might ask. Certainly, you need to adapt your plans, strategies, and actions if changing conditions would affect your project. You will have a far greater ability to adapt to change and stay in control of your plan if you follow the plan. In the helicopter approach, what would happen if conditions changed while you were standing on your flimsy pole at step forty-two?

> Business is like war in one respect. If its grand strategy is correct, any number of tactical errors can be made and yet the enterprise proves successful.
>
> —

You are barely staying upright and now you have to adapt to

a change? By following through with all the steps in your plan, you will:

1. Be prepared to accelerate and adapt to change when it really counts.

2. Make the most efficient use of resources to execute your project.

3. Avoid costly rework and parallel activities.

4. Significantly reduce the risk of failure and increase the assurance of success.

Every time you are tempted to call for that helicopter shortcut, make the choice instead to become a champion and get on with it!

KNOWLEDGE DRIVES VISION:

Remember in Section I we talked about the importance of knowledge in achieving your purpose. Developing a successful strategy to execute your business vision, or purpose, also requires a lot of knowledge. You must know exactly what you are going to do, why, how, and when, and then align all of that with your vision across every aspect of your business in order to have any chance of success.

You might say: "What if I don't know what I need to know?" There you go with that "What if... ?" question again. Instead, ask yourself what questions you must ask that would enable you to develop an informed business strategy. There are simply hundreds of questions to ask and as a CEO you should never stop asking them. That way you can always stay ahead of issues and take actions to keep moving forward.

Several key questions are worth asking at the beginning of a venture, and preferably, you will be asking them repeatedly each year. I call them the "20 What" Questions. You will find them helpful in clarifying for you the key components of information you will need to develop a business strategy. Of course, the ultimate answer to some of these questions could be the result of a large volume of work, but that is what we call "execution" and it follows this section.

THE 20 "WHAT?" QUESTIONS:

1. What outcome do you promise for the customers who benefit from your product or service? The answer to this will define your vision.

2. What reputation do you want for your business in the future?

3. What services or products does your business provide to your customers?

4. What experience should your team and your customers expect to enjoy in a relationship with your business?

5. What key benefits can your customers receive from your business?

6. What specific needs and people does your business address?

7. What size is the potential buying population?

8. What will you do to reach them to make them aware of your business?

9. What will you do to deliver your product to them?

10. What would make them buy from you rather than someone else?

11. What would they be willing to pay you for your product?

12. What does it cost to deliver and service the product?

13. What other companies offer similar products and why they are successful?

14. What have you invented that may be worth patenting?

15. What have you created that may be worth copyright or trademark protection?

16. What manufacturing process will you use to develop and produce the product?

17. What form of company will best serve your business?

18. What alliances with other companies will be helpful to your business?

19. What core team expertise do you need on your management team?

20. What will it cost to get the company and products ready for launch?

CHAPTER 8:

Leadership

Leadership has to do with direction. Management has to do with the speed, coordination and logistics in going in that direction. The WORKERS are chopping their way through the jungle. The MANAGERS are coordinating, making sure the tools are sharp, etc.

The LEADERS climb a tree and shout: "Wrong Jungle!!"

The MANAGERS shout back: "Be quiet! We're making progress!"

—Anonymous

That reminds me of an exercise we performed regularly during army training many years ago. The instructor would tell one of the soldiers to run to the top of a hill, collect a small rock and bring it back to him. As the panting trooper returned, a barrage of insults for bringing back the "wrong rock" met him. He then had to run back up the hill, put this rock back in its place and bring back another one. The consequence for his 'poor judgment' was that the entire platoon would join him in running up the hill and back together.

Of course, we all knew this was a game and it seemed rather pointless at the time. However, the clever part of this game is that it plays against our desire to avoid running up the hill no matter how inevitable that would be. Quickly we would realize that we all needed to get up and down this hill in an orderly and efficient manner. Soon, the stronger among us would help the weaker soldiers along so that we would leave no stragglers behind. It did not take long before we began to see, through many similar exercises, that we could accomplish a lot more as a unit than we might have believed.

> Leadership is not magnetic personality—that can just as well be a glib tongue. It is not making friends and influencing people—that is flattery. Leadership is lifting a person's vision to higher sights, the raising of a person's performance to a higher standard, the building of a personality beyond its normal limitations.
> —Peter F. Drucker

Think of someone you know and admire as a great leader. Now list the key strengths or characteristics of that person that were worthy of your admiration. The truly great leaders tend to share one common attribute that propels them to great heights while building huge flocks of loyal followers. You may recognize this attribute as being "grounded", in spite of their achievements. Alternatively, maybe you can see that they have the ability to connect with "regular" people while they soar to new heights. You may also notice that they have a predisposition to acknowledge openly the contributions of others to their success.

All strong leaders know that no matter how high they rise, they need to have a strong foundation. This solid foundation has at its roots the principles of integrity and honesty and perhaps more importantly, humility.

> Do you wish to rise? Begin by descending. Do you plan a tower that will pierce the clouds? Lay first the foundation of humility.
> —Saint Augustine of Hippo.

Some people may be puzzled that we are talking about "rising" and "piercing the clouds" in the same sentence as the word humility. Surely to achieve such success requires a bold conqueror who bravely leads the charge to obliterate any obstacle along the way. What place is there for humility in that? Too often, we equate humility with submissive and weak behavior. That is not the humility of successful leaders.

> The first test of a truly great man is his humility. By humility, I don't mean doubt of his powers or hesitation in speaking his opinion, but merely an understanding of the relationship of what he can say and what he can do.
>
> —John Ruskin

Humility in leadership entails a person's honest and open assessment of his or her own abilities, and the contribution of relationships with others. Being humble does not imply in any way that we doubt our own abilities, nor refrain from asserting our ideas, nor boldly charge forward. Humble leadership requires great strength of character, and it can produce even greater results for the leader and the people under their charge.

To be an effective leader that will earn the loyalty and dedication of people who will follow you regardless of how challenging the journey, you need to earn their respect. The rungs of the ladder to success comprise the backs of the people who lifted you to the top. Tread lightly and never forget who got you to where you are. Many people get to the top by stepping roughly on the people around and below them. The people on whose backs they stomped will never forget the way they were treated. When all those broken backs hear the call to rescue that leader, what will they do? How strong is that leader's ladder? Those leaders are paper tigers, not real leaders.

A statement made by an outstanding leader on the day of his release from prison exemplified this principle of servant leadership:

> I stand here before you not as a prophet but as a humble servant of you, the people. Your tireless and heroic sacrifices have made it possible for me to be here today. I therefore place the remaining years of my life in your hands.
>
> —Nelson Mandela

With statements and an attitude like this, Mandela instantly earned the respect of all of the people of South Africa, enabling him to lead the country peacefully into a new era.

Note that we use the phrase "earn their respect". What happens when a leader engages in a lot of self-promotion to convince the world at large that they are great? Nobody is fooled by that, and worse, if the individual really is a lousy leader, then this publicity will only enhance and reinforce that impression.

> What kills a skunk is the publicity it gives itself.
>
> —Abraham Lincoln

Instead of focusing all their energy trying to convince people that that they are great, why not just be great? If you do good things for people, they will appreciate it and they will most likely tell someone else how you have helped them. You would be that much greater if other people were singing your praises. Earn their respect and acknowledge their contributions and their value to your success.

But all leaders have weaknesses, you say. Are we suggesting that leaders admit their weaknesses and potentially expose themselves to attack? In a word, "yes". That is not to say that you simply admit to many things you cannot do as a leader, and that you make mistakes and fall on your sword. What is the bet that someone in the team you lead, or perhaps an outsider, is quite strong at something that you consider a personal weakness. Enlist their support and together you will produce a better result and demonstrate to the team that you know how to lead.

If you make a mistake, acknowledge it, remain focused on your mission and goals, and get the team to help you move forward. This will build trust and strong team bonds that will allow you and the team to ride safely over the many speed bumps that are to come in your business journey.

LEADERSHIP ATTITUDE:

In Section I, I said that everything starts with the attitude of the leader. This section on leadership illustrates the issue clearly. Imagine if your personal attitude was weak. Your own beliefs and fears rise to the surface and you have no confidence that you can accomplish anything. Aside from not developing your own potential, what kind of leader would you make? You cannot fake or pretend leadership. It is not a mask you can wear to cover your own weaknesses and somehow inspire others to greatness. Rather it is an attitude that stems from a belief in one's self, a belief in the potential in others, and a belief in achieving the vision.

> The chief executive who knows his strengths and weaknesses as a leader is likely to be far more effective than the one who remains blind to them. He also is on the road to humility, that priceless attitude of openness to life that can help a manager absorb mistakes, failures, or personal shortcomings.
>
> —John Adair

SECTION III:
TOOLS REQUIRED TO EXECUTE

CHAPTER 9:

Introducing the Tools for Execution

There are three key elements that we need in order to fuel the business concept that you have developed. The first is capital, the second is systems, and the third is people.

There are two types of capital.

The most important is intellectual capital. That goes right back to YOU. The invention, the processes, the ideas, and the leadership you (and your team) bring to the business are key components that help you acquire the second form of capital, and that is CASH. If your attitude, and therefore leadership, is weak, then you will not be effective at raising cash.

Why are YOU the intellectual capital? The first thing an investor wants to be sure of is that you represent someone they can believe in; someone who will develop a successful business and generate the maximum return for their investment.

Why do you need CASH capital? Cash is required to develop the systems that will allow you to execute your strategy. All of the processes you described in your business strategy need to be developed so that your company has the ability to grow efficiently without adding cost, and with the ability to support rapid growth. Then ultimately, you will need people to help run your business and to support your customers. If your leadership is weak, then these people will ultimately not be productive and your business will fail.

CHAPTER 10:
Capital

INTELLECTUAL CAPITAL

The first and most important form of capital starts with an idea. You can clearly define, develop, and protect ideas by patents, copyrights, and trademarks. Not only can legal processes protect ideas, but you can also protect secret formulas as trade secrets. Some ideas or inventions may have a shorter useful life or may better serve broader applications through the patent process. Yet others may be creative works ranging from writing to art to training manuals that are protected by copyrights. When ideas reach this stage of definition, we call them intellectual property.

As such, a financial value can be assigned to them. Why? Because ideas can be converted into products and services that make a huge difference in the lives and business of millions of people. This potential will determine the ultimate value of the idea and the intellectual property that someone may be willing to invest in, or license, to create and market products.

> Thought, not money, is the real business capital.
>
> —Harvey S. Firestone

Right next to the idea, the next form of capital that will attract investments is the brainpower of the inventor and the leadership team that will develop and manage the process of converting the idea into a profitable venture. An idea without the relevant intellect, knowledge, and leadership to champion it through the long and arduous journey to success is just a dream. An idea surrounded by the right team of people who are committed to its fruition has substantial potential.

Venture firms and other investors in small, high growth businesses will almost always tell you that the number one thing they look for in a new investment opportunity is the leadership team. Imagine that you have fear and doubt about the potential for your great idea. Imagine that you do not believe that anyone would take you seriously as the leader of your enterprise. What do you suppose will happen when you enter the room with a venture capitalist or investment banker, or even a high net worth individual?

Before you even share with them any information about your idea, your plans to develop it, and what you need from them, they have already decided what type of leader you are. The fear, doubt, or uncertainty you feel hangs over you like a veil, masking the true potential behind it. Perceptive investors will detect this and decide that you are not an example of a leader in which they would invest.

This may seem unfair, but it serves as a natural and often very effective filtering mechanism to eliminate one of the biggest risks associated with a new venture–YOU. Once again, we see that the model requires all elements, at all levels, to integrate and align. If your attitude is not confident, committed, passionate, filled with belief, and demonstrating the knowledge to execute your dream, then you will struggle to convince anyone else to invest in it.

Are you trying to sell an idea for a project or business? Do you need to raise investment capital or obtain corporate funding? If you need to gain investor, executive, and peer support for your project, you must convince them quickly of your confidence. You will not be successful if you are a nervous wreck, or if you are not fully prepared. Many people get anxious about this, but they do not really know why or what to do about it.

One of the biggest contributors to this anxiety is too much focus on YOU. What does this mean? Some ways that you can sabotage a good business opportunity include:

- Putting your personal needs in front of your passion for the opportunity.

- Believing that you are asking someone to give you money because right now your needs are great. Instead, you should be convincing them of an opportunity to make or save money because of your project proposal.

- Allowing your fear of rejection to restrain your enthusiasm and confidence.

- Poorly thought-out logic for how you propose to address the opportunity.

- Insufficient supporting information to validate your assertions.

- Denial about the competitive threats that already exist.

- Lack of understanding about the risks to the project and potential mitigation strategies.

The investor or decision maker will evaluate your presentation based on how effectively you convince them about the outcome you are proposing. Is it desirable, achievable, and are you committed to seeing it through? This requires a balance of both elements to be successful. That is, a balance between the opportunity, and you. Imagine the scale that must balance with the weight of the opportunity on one side and the weight of your commitment on the other.

On the opportunity side, you must convince them that the opportunity is worth pursuing. You have a clear and compelling long-term vision for what the outcome will be. You understand the problem thoroughly. You can identify the people, and a significant number of them, that acknowledge they need a solution to the problem. You understand how to reach these people and get your solution to them. You are aware of the competition and the reasons why your solution is better. You have a clear logical process and model for proving the return on investment this project will produce. You have assembled a strong team of people to help you accomplish the project. You understand some of the key risks involved and the potential strategies for reducing them.

On the "YOU" side, you must convince them that you believe in this project and the outcome you seek to create. You are confident that the solution, the team, and the proposed project will be executed successfully and will deliver the outcomes you are seeking. You are passionate about the vision and the potential that this project has to make the difference you believe is possible. You are committed and dedicated to achieving this regardless of the bumps in the road that will appear. You must believe without hesitation that this is the best solution, and that it will succeed. You must be courageous enough to present and defend your project to just about anyone, putting your own ego and fears aside.

Focusing on the opportunity side allows the magic to happen. Specifically, you need to address the following considerations:

- Build the case for why this is a great opportunity, and why the outcome is so compelling.

- Articulate your understanding of the business model that will be required.

- Demonstrate that you understand how to build the roadmap to success.

- Illustrate the risks and challenges that this project will face.

- Demonstrate your understanding of the proposed actions to mitigate them.

- Share the competency, experience, and overall ability of the team you have assembled to execute the project successfully.

- Convince them that you have thoroughly assessed the risks and the resources needed.

Show them that you understand the connection between their investment, the manner in which you will return that investment, and how their investment will multiply.

Leading with the opportunity side automatically builds the value of the "YOU" side as:

- Your knowledge of the subject increases as you develop the business case and the logic flow from investment to returns.

- Your confidence increases as you develop strategies to manage risk, recruit the best possible team, and assure that the design of your model is sound.

- Your belief and commitment to the project grows as your confidence increases in the project, the business case, and the team that can execute it.

- Your courage will grow as you present the case, along with your knowledge, confidence and belief in the project.

> Courage is rarely reckless or foolish... courage usually involves a highly realistic estimate of the odds that must be faced.
> —Margaret Truman

By focusing diligently on the opportunity, you will automatically accrue knowledge, confidence, belief, commitment, and courage on the "you" side of the scale. This is exactly what is required to balance the scale, and you focusing any energy on it, other than by developing the opportunity side, cannot place it there. The point is that the "you" side is not about you at all. Instead, it is what the audience perceives about you as you communicate the story about the opportunity. They will clearly see your passion and commitment for the opportunity and the outcomes it can generate.

If presenting to a group audience is intimidating, then the best thing to do is practice. Assemble a group of people who are close and friendly and ask them to give you honest feedback on your presentation. Deliver your presentation in front of a video camera and play it back to yourself. This will help you with delivery of the message and with timing: learning to anticipate where questions might arise. Remember: you are selling an opportunity for the decision maker regarding a return on investment outcome first. You are not selling yourself or soliciting help to save you from any difficulty. This is not purely about confidence.

> Confidence is going after Moby Dick in a rowboat, and taking the tartar sauce with you. A bullfighter who goes in the ring with mustard on his sword.
>
> —Zig Ziglar

By focusing on the opportunity, you can develop courage in the knowledge that your business case and strategy are sound. Once again, we see that your attitude, at the center of the first gear in Section I, plays a huge role in your ability to influence and motivate others to support your business—in this case, investors.

This leads us to the key form of capital that will be the biggest contributor to converting your well thought out strategies and plans into a successful business venture—cash. You need cash to pay people, to develop and manufacture products, to market and distribute products and services, to pay sales people, to pay the rent, lights and insurance, and the list goes on. The strategies that you developed in Section II will require systems to execute your business. Systems will allow your business to perform and grow while maintaining operational and customer service without increasing spending or reducing throughput.

You need cash to secure the right people in the right roles as ultimately the success of your business will require people to execute effectively. You need cash to develop and manufacture your product and to take it to market. You need cash to smooth over the timing issues that every business invariably faces when the timing of receivables and payables temporarily becomes unsynchronized. People and suppliers expect payment regardless of whether your customers have paid you yet. Cash bridges those gaps. Cash flow, created by a steady increase in funds from operating the business after paying for expenses, is the grease that keeps the business running and allows new investments to be made to support growth.

Cash flow is the grease that keeps the business running

CAPITAL SEQUENCING

Assume you have made it past the first hurdle in convincing investors that you are the caliber of leaders they seek. It will be helpful to have a clear understanding of the process and important milestones involved in acquiring investment capital during the key startup phases of your venture. This sequence and the conversations with investors revolve around creating the right balance and expectations between managing risk and developing value.

> Money is the seed of money, and the first guinea is sometimes more difficult to acquire than the second million.
>
> —Jean Jacques Rousseau

This is very true. I've heard many people who have invented a new product or service say that they visited investors who want seventy percent of their business plus they want to insert their own management team. The general reaction to these investors is that they are sharks waiting to prey on defenseless people. But is that really the case? Let us look at this from the point of view of the investor. At the start of any venture, when the idea is still fresh and being formed, the risks involved in converting the idea into a profitable business are at their highest. At this stage, you have not proven that you can convert the idea into a product and sell that product to enough people to make a good return.

If you are asking the investor to assume the majority of the risk at this early stage, then clearly they want to receive the majority of the reward. Likewise, they will want to put people and processes in place that they have high confidence in to execute the business successfully. That is, if you have not convinced them that you are the caliber of leader they want, then they want to reduce the risk that you represent. This is also why it is often more difficult to raise the initial seed funding for a new venture than it may be for an established business looking to grow. It is all about risk and value.

It is all about risk and value

MILESTONES

The key milestones that a new idea, or venture, need to follow in order to reduce risk and increase business value, are:

1. Develop a basic business strategy around the idea and vision for the product or service

2. Protect the intellectual property of the invention

3. Build a working prototype

4. Build a repeatable finished manufactured product

5. Run field trials with customers

6. Sell the product to paying customers

STRATEGY AND ROADMAP

First, we need to convert the idea into a strategy and a roadmap of key milestones designed to demonstrate progress and reduce the risks in stages as the business progresses. As the risks are reduced, the value is increased, and the likelihood of attracting investors increases. As the value increases, you also sell fewer shares in your company at a higher price, thereby avoiding the potential loss of the majority of your business.

The strategy and roadmap on their own are not particularly effective at raising large amounts of capital, but they will serve to demonstrate to seed round individuals that you have a thorough plan for execution. You will be able to communicate that you understand how this idea can convert into a business. If you are at the very beginning stage of your business venture, then developing a strategy is a key first step. In addition to understanding the model described in this book and creating a plan and roadmap to develop the blueprint for your business, a basic strategy needs to include:

- **Vision**—the purpose for the business. The future outcome the business is intending to create for its customers.

- **Mission**—the overarching goal for the business. This is a statement clarifying what the business does, for whom, and to what end (i.e., connected to the vision).

- **Values**—the guiding principles governing the behavior of the people in the business. These are not simply words like honesty and teamwork. Instead, they are statements about expected behavior with regard to such key words.

- **Value propositions**—the benefits the business provides to its customers. What problems or challenges do the customers of this business face? What are the key benefits our products and services provide to address those problems? Why are we better or different from other suppliers? These questions lead to a set of statements about the value you propose to customers.

- **Long-term objectives**—the measurements of success five years from now. These statements define the accomplishments in measurable terms in several key facets of the business. These include finances (revenue and profit), operations, people, leadership, marketing, technology and others that may be significant to your specific venture.

- **Short-term priorities**—the work we know needs to be done in the next nine months. Typically, this can be a long and detailed list. Without assigning dates and owners responsible for each item, entrepreneurs easily become overwhelmed or lose track of the bigger picture.

This basic strategy creates a foundation or platform on which everything else in your business can be built, including products and services, brand strategies, marketing, sales, and services, and even management and employee recruiting. The strategy serves as a filter for every choice or decision to assure the optimal alignment and increase your potential for success. After your own attitude, this is the first step in reducing risk.

Second, we need to protect the intellectual property of the invention. Patents can potentially protect new product and service designs, functionality, and methods. A patent attorney can conduct a thorough patent search to ensure your invention is unique enough and defensible. Then they can help you to define the patent in broad yet specific enough terms to protect your invention and reduce the risk of knock-offs. Patents can expire after seventeen years, so you will need to make sure your business achieves the return you desire from that invention before it becomes public domain information.

Creative works, including writing, music, lyrics, art, training manuals, graphic designs and symbols all have the potential for protection by copyright registration. Any such material that is central to distinguishing the product, service, or other aspects of the business needs registration. Simply assigning a Copyright © notice and symbol on the product is not sufficient. That works well for text on web sites or other marketing material, but not for products themselves. Copyrights can last as long as the creator plus seventy years and even more depending on circumstances.

Names and symbols of products and of your company will benefit from trademark registration. After searching for potential conflicts with other trademarks, immediately add the ™ symbol after the name or symbol and then proceed with registration. Trademark enforcement is most effective by demonstrating usage. If you register a trademark and never use it, you will risk losing it if a competitor chooses to use it and does so for any period without a challenge. You must renew trademark registrations every five years to demonstrate that the marque is indeed still in use.

Certain products may be the result of complex or secret formulas that are difficult to replicate. Their importance to the business means they may be better managed as trade secrets. Coca Cola is a good example of this. If the Coke formula had been patented, it would long ago have become public domain knowledge and the company would have lost its most important asset. Although the generic ingredients are listed on the side of a can of soda, without knowing precisely how, and in what proportions those ingredients are delivered into the mix, the formula cannot easily be duplicated.

These basic steps in protecting your intellectual property establish the first elements of tangible value for your business. Achieving this can demonstrate that you may indeed have something unique to offer that others cannot duplicate exactly for some time. The risk attached to the business at this stage is still very high, as the value created thus far is primarily on paper. That is, you have not yet proven you can make or sell the product. Seed round investors may be more motivated based on achieving this second step as you now have a strategy and a protected invention.

Third, you will need to build a working prototype of your product or service. The prototype does not have to be a polished, finely tuned, manufactured product. However, it does have to work. It is a demonstration that the invention or solution can in fact be created to perform as you intended. For physical products, plan to include high quality engineering or product design drawings to illustrate to potential users and investors what that ultimate product will be.

Drawings also communicate a sense of realness that a rough working prototype may not. For service businesses, the prototype may be a documented process, a basic software product, or similar artifacts that can demonstrate the actual workings of your solution. This third step moves you along the risk/value progression by showing that the idea or invention may be feasible. You may be able to attract first round investment funding to begin the development and preparation of your product for the marketplace in earnest.

Fourth, you will need to demonstrate that the product can be manufactured in high volume, with quality, and at the right price points to produce a profit. Ideally, the product design will be complete and a first run produced by a professional manufacturer capable of supporting the initial sales volume. However, achieving this first production run may require funding not available during the startup process. In that case, manufacturing drawings, written quotes from manufacturers, and potentially manufacturer-produced prototypes are an option.

For service businesses, this stage demonstrates that you have fully documented your solution, your software development is functionally complete, and a competent person is available to deliver the service. This fourth step increases the value of your business by reducing the risk of not producing your product or service in a reliable and cost effective fashion.

Fifth, you will need to have prospective customers evaluate your product as hands-on users or through formal evaluation methods. For many products, including software and services, this step integrates into step four above as the customer's feedback during the development cycle factors into the process to assure the product meets customer needs and expectations. This is achievable for certain physical products during the prototype stage as well. The goal is to have prospective trial customers who are indeed interested in being actual customers for the final product.

Large customers with recognizable names, or large numbers of trial customers, will provide valuable testimony to the value and benefits of your product. Have them write positive remarks about their experience on their letterhead. Also have them, as appropriate, write letters of intent on their letterhead regarding their desire to deploy your product when it is "production ready". This step is really important in reducing the risk, as you will for the first time in the process, demonstrate that prospective customers are validating your product and clearly indicating their willingness to purchase it.

Sixth and last, you will need to have actual paying customers for your product or service. Start with one, and then add another. Do not be impatient about this stage. It is tempting to want to go fast before you are ready. This is the launch phase. You may need substantial capital to establish the business, the technology and operations infrastructure, and the sales and marketing initiatives to launch and grow your business to its potential.

Having paying customers, and the more of them the better, is the biggest magnet for investment capital that you can create. At this stage, you will have the potential to receive funding from a variety of sources. Since the value of your business is at an all time high, you will not only have greater potential to attract funding but also to sell a smaller portion of the company to investors.

CHAPTER 11:

Systems

Civilization advances by extending the number of important operations that we can perform without thinking.
— Alfred North Whitehead

In other words, or rather, a word: systems. Business ventures advance by developing, enhancing, and maintaining operational systems that support the execution of the activities of the business with little or no human intervention. This frees creative human minds to focus on far more valuable innovations and problem solving activities. Investing capital to develop automated systems, process, and perhaps even outsource functions to other entities will create a growth engine for the company.

Systems can take on more and more work and process it efficiently with only marginal incremental costs. What are these systems? Look back to your strategy from the business layer of the model. You have determined the product development, manufacturing, service delivery, logistics, marketing, distribution and many more strategies to execute to assure your success. In addition to these systems, administrative processes for financial management and human resource management also need to take place effectively.

If you rely heavily on people to conduct most of the work in your business, then you will discover that growth comes at a great expense. Hiring individuals can be costly and time consuming.

Furthermore, people have limited capacity to do work so the incremental investment is higher. People need training; they are more prone to errors, and they tend to need time off for vacation, illness, and family care. People are typically the highest single expense item on most income statements.

Well-designed and managed operating systems can defer much of this expense while providing an efficient growth platform to support rapid and sustainable profitability. I am not suggesting you never hire people in your business. In the end, people run businesses, and successful business relationships depend on the people who establish them. People can ingeniously solve problems, invent new products, serve and support customers and generally improve the operation of your business in ways that automated systems cannot. The emphasis here is on work that is performed repeatedly, reliably, accurately, and in high volume without requiring change or innovation to the processes themselves.

A system does not necessarily have to be a large complex computerized business process. A simple procedure guide or manual on how to do essential tasks around the office is an example of a basic system that saves people time, assures consistency, and allows new people to come into the company and follow the correct procedures from the start. That does not mean the manuals or guides will not change, and indeed they should change as the business evolves and processes develop and grow. Then, as certain work categories become repetitious and require the accomplishment of large volumes of work, computer automation becomes essential.

Look for industry associations or standards bodies that may have produced an industry standard for your area of business. Learning how to adopt and support those standards can significantly enhance your operation by streamlining processes in such a way that enhance your ability to relate to suppliers, partners, and customers. Manysuch standards are developed based on the experience and knowledge of large corporations who have years of experience and teams of engineers developing them. That gives you the ability to achieve the same level of quality with a minimal investment. Of course, as a small enterprise, you need to assess what standards are relevant and necessary for your business.

Another important area where systems are very helpful is in the area of regulatory and accounting compliance. Systems provide standardized methods for complying with regulations that can protect your company from liability from violations or questionable practices. Some areas, like accounting, are the same across all businesses, whereas others dealing with security and privacy and government reporting may be more specific to the nature of your business. Seeking the advice of legal, accounting, and IT experts can be invaluable.

With the right attitude, systems can be developed and evolved. From the very beginning of the business, develop a bias toward understanding what work you may manage more effectively by a system. Set an expectation before you hire a new person to do work, that you have assessed the work that needs to be done, to be sure that a system could not handle the work better. This may not eliminate the need to hire someone, but it will make the business more productive. As the business grows, this attitude will produce significant returns as more and more work is performed efficiently by systems you put in place along the way.

You may not be sure what systems you may need at first or if you need any at all. Here are some questions to help you focus attention on specific target areas for operational efficiencies and decision-making improvements. This list is by no means a complete list of questions covering all operations and systems required by an enterprise. However, they do point to common challenges faced by many small and emerging businesses.

1. Following the 80:20 rule that suggests 80 percent of your business comes from 20 percent of your customers, how quickly can you list your top 20 percent ranked by sales over the last six months?

2. What are the monthly and quarterly operating budget and actual spending numbers for your business?

3. Can you take on new products without adding to or modifying your operations or systems?

4. Do you know exactly what specific projects are costing you, including the time of people involved?

5. What was the value of new sales directly driven by a specific promotion program?

6. Who are your top sales prospects? Have you ranked them by the progress you have made with them—e.g., initial contact, meeting, proposal, contract, etc.?

7. Do you keep all sales prospect communication in an organized electronic system so they can be accessed instantly?

8. How much time is spent re-entering accounting or customer sales information into different systems?

9. Is your retail store front, and your web store integrated with your accounting and inventory management systems so all financial and customer information can be reported from one system?

10. How quickly could you produce monthly or quarterly financial reports for your business?

11. Are customers able to re-visit their web store orders on your web site? Can they track order progress or make order/ customer data adjustments?

12. Are you able to issue competitive tenders to your suppliers on line, and get them to respond with best prices?

13. Can your remote sales and service people access customer and order information over the internet?

14. Do you have a standard performance review process for ALL employees?

15. How many people were absent for how many hours last month? What was the reason for the absence?

16. What government regulations are your business required to follow? Have your employees been trained accordingly?

CHAPTER 12:

People

A man was walking along a country road and he came to the beginning of a steep hill. At the bottom of the hill, he came upon a farmer with a wagon heavily loaded with farm produce. A tiny donkey was hitched up to the yoke in front of the farm cart. The man asked the farmer how he could possibly expect that little donkey to pull such a huge load up the hill. The farmer responded by yelling out, "Pull Benny, pull!", and then "Pull, Jackie, pull!", and finally "Pull Amos, pull!" Confused, the man asked the farmer why he had just called his donkey three different names. The farmer told him that the donkey was blind. He said that if he thought there were two other donkeys pulling alongside him he pulled a lot harder. That is how he got the little donkey to pull the wagon up the hill.

Why would the donkey pull harder when he thinks he has a team working with him? It could be because he feels more confident that the team will be able to get the job done, rather than attempting to do it alone. Simply knowing that others are supporting you in your endeavor can be a huge motivating and encouraging force. This force will put wind in your sails to help you to cruise right on past all of the doubts that come along and challenge your confidence. Challenges like the huge pile of work, the complexity of the job, the breadth and depth of knowledge required, your own inexperience, and on and on. Imagine a team supporting you with all of those issues. You are immediately likely to feel more confident that you can execute and overcome all of these issues.

Accountability contributes significantly to team motivation. Individuals sometimes feel more accountable to other people than they do to themselves. How many people do you know that go to a fitness club or gym to work out because there are trainers and other exercisers who hold them accountable for their progress? If you believe that other people have made a commitment to support you, you are inclined to want to prove to them that their trust and confidence are well vested in you.

This is like an inflation proofing mechanism. Say your confidence is challenged and you look around at your supporters. They are all cheering you on, or waiting expectantly for the next thing you are going to do, or even rolling up their sleeves and pitching in to help. You are more likely to buckle down and get on with it, despite the obstacles. You will pull harder, just like the farmer's donkey.

> Individual commitment to a group effort -- that is what makes
> a team work, a company work, a society work, a civilization work.
> —Vince Lombardi

Even if the responsibility for your work or project is yours alone, having a team of support allows you to make a commitment to it as though it were a group effort.

Diversity is another key contributor to team motivation—and my personal favorite. It does not matter whether you are the leader of a large enterprise organization or a sole proprietor of a small home based business. If your business depends exclusively on your own brainpower for everything you do, you are severely limiting your capacity. No matter how smart you are, you simply cannot outthink a team in all the aspects of a complex business undertaking.

Do not underestimate the value of any insight you can get from the most unlikely sources either. I regularly share new business ideas with my seventeen-year-old son. I am always impressed by the level of understanding and the insights and creativity he is able to apply to things you might think he knows nothing about. Each of us has people around us that would be equally willing to share their thoughts and ideas if we were more willing to be open to receiving them.

People at the lowest levels in an organization often have a clearer understanding of a specific issue. Their perspective is not clouded with everything else that needs to be done in the company. Sometimes the solution is simpler than we think it might be. There's a story about a gym that provided high-end shampoo in the showers. Clients were so grateful for the luxury that they helped themselves to the bottles, taking them home with them. Management held committee meetings, a security specialist was called in, all to no effect. One day the CEO was in the shower when the cleaner was there. He discussed the problem with the cleaner, who came up with the perfect solution. "Take the tops off the bottles." Problem solved. Nobody wanted shampoo leaking all over their gym clothes. Humans have a tendency to complicate things. If we do not understand them, it must be because they are very complicated and so we assume we need to engineer complex solutions.

Sometimes our ego gets in the way. We shy away of asking other people for their thoughts and ideas because we do not want to appear vulnerable and not totally in control of everything. The person who values input from a diverse range of people, listens to them, and uses that input to make wise and sound decisions, is indeed more in control of their destiny than one who believes they need to do it all by themselves.

Strength lies in differences, not in similarities.

—Stephen Covey

In a large corporation, you have lots of peers and subordinates to help you think things through and to provide creative ideas and solutions to problems. Entrepreneurs who do not have this built-in resource need to reach out and find people who they see as advisors in some form or another. The relationship could be formal, as in a board member role, or it could be casual and built on a loose arrangement with a diverse range of individuals. The relationship can even include family members and other social peers. A hundred diverse ideas will beat twenty of your own any day of the week. Those are good odds. Why would you bet against them? As a team, you will pull harder, think smarter, and dramatically increase the odds of success in your favor.

> Coming together is a beginning, staying together is progress, and working together is success.
>
> —Henry Ford

LEADERSHIP ATTITUDES

In Sections I, II and III, we talked about the role attitude plays in defining your potential, your leadership capacity, and your ability to raise capital. If your attitude is weak, your leadership will be weak, and your people will not be motivated to achieve your vision. People need to be inspired to achieve the vision and align themselves with a purpose bigger than themselves. If they are led by a leader that clearly demonstrates his/her commitment and passion to that same purpose, then they will rise to the promise that is being made to the customer. It all starts with your attitude, and it could end with your attitude as well.

SECTION IV:
MEASURING PERFORMANCE

CHAPTER 13:

Introducing Measurement

Clearly, each gear or layer in this system can function within its own context, whether it is YOU, your Business Concept, or the Tools for Execution. Yet all gears and all elements are required to integrate, synchronize, and cooperate with each other. This produces a complete model that is capable of defining and managing a business successfully. There are also clear dependencies between elements of the different layers in the model. If one specific area is weak, the implications for the rest of the business are clearly visible. A weakness in one element, particularly "leadership", ripples through the entire business model.

Let us reexamine the question, "what do I do next?" The answer depends on where your business is in its state of development or maturity, how well aligned you are to your purpose, and what the vision for your business is. The answer may also depend on the current state of any of the elements in your business gear model. Wherever you start, you now have a better understanding of the bigger picture, and a much clearer context for understanding what to do next and why. You will also have a better understanding of how your next steps will affect the overall business, and what other actions need to be taken as a result. This model can be a guide for any new venture or newly created organization to put their entire enterprise into the context of the big picture.

If you cannot measure it, you cannot improve it.

—Lord Kelvin

Existing businesses could use this model as a control panel of sorts. Measures, reports, and indicators attached to each element of the model allow for periodic assessments and corrections in the businesses. Of course, the real measure of business performance comes from acquiring profitable customer relationships. Everything you do in the business, as illustrated by the functional model of gears, must align to deliver the vision and mission of your company to your customers.

As a measurement tool, you would start on the outside of the model by examining customers first. In addition to customer relationships, adding partners, channels and suppliers is also important. These relationships help to complete the business model by providing specific services, expertise, or the ability to reach customers. With this complete overview of the basic anatomy of the business anatomy, you are now prepared to look at it from the outside.

CHAPTER 14:

Customers

Why do we start measuring our business performance by examining customers first? I occasionally meet entrepreneurs who have succeeded in selling their product or service to several customers. They now have a successful small business. Then they meet an erudite consultant and often conclude that they need to stop whatever they are doing so they can raise capital first. The logic being that without the capital the company simply cannot grow effectively. Well, that is only half-right, but it is a potentially extremely dangerous choice.

> Every company's greatest assets are its customers, because without customers there is no company.
>
> —Michael Leboeuf

Your first priority should always be to service your existing customers and sell your product or service to the next. Customers are the source of all income into your business, and income is the source of all cash flow and profits from ongoing operations. Cash flow and profits allow you to deliver a return to your investors and plow back much needed cash to fuel growth. If you need to raise capital, the most potent risk reducing and value creation tool is a growing list of paying customers.

Measuring your performance with your customers is not a quarterly or even monthly operations review process. A LOT can go wrong between reviews. This must be a discipline built into the processes of the company and it must be included in regular weekly executive reviews.

Some important factors to consider regarding customer measurements include:

1. What current customer relationships are at risk? Why? What will you do immediately to correct the situation?

   Start with existing customers because they are the lifeblood of your business. The cost of acquiring new customers can be several times the cost of selling something new to an existing customer. You will also need these customers to be good references to help you gain new customer relationships. This is not an exercise in targeting and assigning blame to an individual in your company for the situation that has developed. The focus must be on the issue at hand and the solutions that need to be implemented to resolve them.

2. What new customers were acquired? Why did they buy from you?

   What is the status of delivery, shipment, project management, etc., to convert the relationship from a new sale to a happy customer? Remember: first impressions are lasting impressions. If you get this new customer relationship off to a good start, you will reap a long lasting profitable relationship. You will also gain a solid reference to help accelerate sales growth. Knowing why they buy from you also helps you to better position yourself against those competitors in the future.

3. What sales prospects did you lose? Why did you lose them? What competitor(s) won the sale?

What specific reasons did the customer give as to why they chose them versus you? Understanding this information allows you to adjust your sales approach, enhance your product offering, and improve your competitive position when dealing with those competitors in the future.

4. What new and/or large prospects do you have that need special attention to close the sale?

What specific actions are you planning to maximize your opportunity to close the sale? The pipeline of new prospective customers is the fuel for growth into your company.

5. What are the trends and programs for sales and service performance related to revenue, profitability, sales pipeline trends, marketing and promotions, customer retention and satisfaction?

This analysis can be included in monthly or regular business operations meetings as it focuses internally and not directly in the path of immediate actions that can affect customer relationships.

> Rule Number 1: Never lose money. Rule Number 2: Never forget rule Number 1.
>
> —Warren Buffett

CHAPTER 15:

Partners

Partners provide opportunities for your business to reach customers that you may not be able to reach without considerable time and expense. Partners can expand the breadth of the solution you provide by combining additional products and services needed by the customer. Partners can enhance your positioning by association with their brand reputation.

When a partner agrees to integrate your product or service into their offerings to their customers, they are making a big commitment. This may indeed include a significant financial and resource commitment. Systems may need to be enhanced to support your product, and people may need to be trained and dedicated to selling and support services. This commitment also includes putting their reputation on the line. If your product disappoints customers for any reason, it will damage your partner's reputation in addition to your own.

For this reason, either partner should never enter into partner relationships lightly. You need to understand exactly what commitments both sides require, and put in place measures and management processes to assure that the relationship is working optimally. The word partner implies collaboration. This means you must treat your partner with respect and learn to appreciate their perspective in addition to communicating your own. This also means honoring commitments that you make to the partner to support them in their efforts with your product or service.

> Demand no more out of your partner than what you are willing to give yourself.
>
> —Martha Quinn

How do you decide what channel partners make sense for your business? A list of helpful questions follows:

1. What customers do they serve?

You want to know specifically what their customer segments are, where they are, how the partner reaches them, and how many of them there are.

2. What value do they add to the overall product or solution the customer buys from them?

They may add services and/or other product components to produce a broader product offering than your product alone.

3. Do they provide a specific value to your business by complementing your own capabilities?

This includes a distribution network that can deliver the product to the customer. It also includes other business services like technical support or other specific business functions that you may lack in order to serve this customer set.

Different customer segments may have very different needs and buying cycles. This increases the need for channel partners who can specifically address these needs for those specific customers.

4. What role does your product play in the overall offerings of the partner?

If your product is not important to them—a "nice to have"—you cannot expect them to dedicate much energy into promoting it successfully. Ideally, your product will be very important to them and their customers.

5. Do you have other channels for reaching the same customers?

If you do have other channels, is channel conflict an issue, or can your product support multiple channels into the same market?

If channel conflict is an issue, do you plan to provide restrictions on customer segments or geographies to remove the conflict?

Your goal is to simplify the buying process for customers as much as possible. This means providing simple choices to make. Even if the product is available through different channels, the choice always seems roughly the same. That is, a choice between you and your competitor, and not a choice between partner A and partner B, with your product being represented quite differently by each. This also means not having too many channels, as that can create negative reactions from the channel partners themselves.

6. What specific commitments is your channel partner willing to make?

These could include sales volumes, training, support resources, marketing and promotion, and technical integration.

7. What specific commitments are you willing to make to support your channel partner?

These include marketing, training, support, technology integration.

8. What management processes are included in the agreement to review financial, operational, and marketing and sales performance?

In addition to assuring that you are measuring performance, regular management reviews also allow you to anticipate and plan for changes that may be needed in the relationship in order to adapt to changes in the marketplace.

CHAPTER 16:

Suppliers

Suppliers play a very important role in completing your product offerings with materials and parts that you need to build them. Suppliers may also have services and operations that can enhance your own operational efficiency. In other words, do not simply look to the supplier to deliver component parts. Instead, establish a collaborative relationship whereby the supplier connects their business with the purpose and mission of your business with your customers.

> Let us ask our suppliers to come and help us to solve our problems
> —W. Edwards Deming

This implies establishing collaborative relationships such that your suppliers develop a comprehensive view of your customer facing systems. This includes the factors influencing demand for your product, and the processes for delivering products to increase efficiency, reduce cost, and reduce the risk of a failure. Clearly, this goes way beyond simply supplying products or component parts. This approach connects the supplier with your business objectives and assures their actions and support systems will be oriented in that direction.

This also means that the relationship contemplates the long-term strategies, plans and trends for your business so that systems adjust to achieve your objectives. The joint relationship can then better address the broader go-to-market issues for the complete delivery value chain, changes in marketplace conditions, and competitor developments. You must ensure that the relationship with the supplier supports your business strategy directly and does not compromise your strategy to fit their existing business models. Doing so would hamper your ability to deliver the products and services that your customers expect. You will then incur great expense attempting to patch up the gaps or differences between the suppliers systems and your own strategy.

As you develop a collaborative relationship with any supplier, make sure you understand the cost and other financial implications of each proposed business model. There are many technology solutions available for managing relationships with suppliers. Treat them as you would any new supplier relationship. That is, make sure that the technology supports your business strategy first, and resist having some attractive package define your strategy for you.

Some useful questions to consider include:

1. How important is the supplier's product to your product offering?

2. Do they have other products that can expand your product offering or open up new markets for you?

3. Do they have operational, delivery, support, or other systems that could support your business strategy directly?

4. What is the cost of each option for integrating their business with your strategy?

5. What is the specific benefit in terms of cost savings or increased sales or more efficient service from this relationship?

6. Is the supplier willing to enter a collaborative relationship whereby they align with your strategy?

7. What alternative suppliers exist for the same products and how do they measure up against these questions?

CHAPTER 17:
Executive Control Panel

Most self-powered vehicles have some kind of control panel, or dashboard, to keep the driver informed of critical information during the journey. Your car dashboard may include dials and gauges to indicate your speed, revolutions per minute of the engine, engine temperature, fuel level, oil pressure, distance covered, tire pressure, and outside air temperature.

These gauges provide important indicators that communicate the health of the vehicle, and other important information that lets the driver anticipate and make important decisions along the way. Decisions like where and when to stop for fuel, or other actions to keep the vehicle operating properly. As the pilot, or leader, of a business, you too will benefit greatly by having access to key performance and measurement information. This information will be critical to your ability to anticipate and make decisions to keep your business operating properly.

I once worked as general manager for a product division of a large technology company. The company held monthly operational reviews with the executive committee, led by the president. The agenda for each general manager's report was the income statement for his or her business division. The primary purpose was to report key developments since the previous month, and to discuss variances from the plan or from performance standards (like inventory turns or customer service costs).

This approach made a lot of sense: the top of the income statement starts with revenue and then works its way down through product costs (manufacturing, distribution and support), to sales and marketing, and then to other general overheads. Revenue, of course, requires a discussion about customers. Therefore, each report began with a review of how the business was doing with regard to sales, retention and so on. These reports came to affectionately be called the "Good, Bad, and Ugly" reports. These reports were quite effective for an operational and financial review. Although it worked well, it was an incomplete assessment. The process did not consider other key aspects of the business that are implicit in this gearbox model.

Like the income statement approach, the gearbox model can serve as the agenda for a quarterly executive review. Starting from the outside of the model the review would begin with customers, partners and suppliers. Then it would shift to the top gear, or execution layer, of the model being capital, systems and people. Next on the list is the business strategy, comprising the vision, strategy and leadership. And, finally, the review centers on the leaders, including attitudes, purposes, and knowledge.

In this way, a review of operational and financial elements combines with a review of vision, strategy, and leadership, and includes the leaders themselves. This process increases awareness of all of the elements required to run the business, their current state, and their impact on other elements. This reveals key dimensions that a pure operational or financial review may not. It also facilitates constant realignments to assure that all elements of the business remain on track and focused on the vision.

Define and monitor key metrics, measurements, and programs for every element on the gearbox model. This creates a more complete executive control panel that allows the leadership of the company to maintain a balanced and holistic perspective of their business. This perspective allows for the fine-tuning of operational and performance efficiencies that keep the business running and well optimized to produce results and not surprises.

As you begin to develop the concept of a control panel, some key questions to consider include:

1. Since we measure customer-related elements first, does the control panel give me a high level but accurate picture of key sales activities, successes, failures for the last month? Once again, systems become important to help you manage your business more effectively.

2. Following the customer related measurements, you will want to measure gross profit, inventory, sales trends, projections for sales and production, staffing, absenteeism, days outstanding for receivables and payables, and customer service metrics like call rates.

3. Once you see a significant variance from your expectations, can you quickly obtain detailed information about specific product sales in specific regions, or via specific distributors and resellers?

4. What specific systems or processes are in place to help assure that you are working with accurate information?

5. Does your control panel include key metrics or measures that align with every key executive or manager organization-wide? This positions each one of them in the context of the overall performance of the company and keeps the entire business visible to all the key managers.

6. Are you able to monitor important performance factors in real time to communicate significant variances when they occur? Some specific examples of operational performance factors worth monitoring include:

- A significant new sales order way above your normal run rate

- A significant customer loss

- A sudden increase in service calls due to a specific product failure or defect

- A sudden increase in manufacturing defects and rejection rates

- Labor shortages due to various factors including illness during flu season

- A sudden increase in delivery schedule for large customers or for a group of customers

- Sales trends below target

- Expense trends above target

- A significant shift in product costs

- If your business relies on international divisions for a significant portion of your business, then you will want to monitor sudden shifts in relevant foreign currency exchange rates.

SECTION V:
COOPERATION

CHAPTER 18:
Competition Blocks Progress

At the very beginning of this book, I said everything begins with attitude. As you execute your business strategy, you may have the attitude that you exist and operate in a competitive world. When this competitive attitude prevails, you naturally draw protective walls around your business. You believe you need to protect your great ideas, systems, and people, so other people don't steal them. You focus on acquiring what you perceive to be scarce resources that you need to keep your business fueled.

Of course, all the partners and suppliers you want to build relationships with are going to operate the same way. The result is that potentially powerful relationships are never established. The trust and unity of purpose and vision are never developed. Unfortunately, most of us are taught that this mode is required for success. It is also, by definition, very difficult to succeed in this mode. It is hardly surprising that so many new business ventures and acquisitions fail.

Protectionism and judgment are two key behavioral attributes of competition that play an important role in breaking down opportunities, rather than building success. In a competitive world, we focus our energy on controlling resources. Since we need resources to produce products, if we can control the supply of the resource we need, then theoretically we can achieve an advantage over our competitors. This means we also work hard to protect our sources for these resources from our competitors.

> The road of isolationism and protectionism ... ends in danger and decline. I am for free commerce with all nations, political connection with none
>
> —Thomas Jefferson

Jefferson was discussing a macroeconomic view, but the sentiment in his statement rings just as true for individual businesses. If you spend all your energy protecting yourself and your resources from others, you achieve a certain measure of success for a while. I say 'a certain measure', as you may temporarily drive others out of the market you are intent on dominating. The challenge comes later on down the road when the resource begins to dry up—as they usually do. Then you will want to learn to evolve into new products, markets, and channels and discover new resources. That is exactly when you will want strong collaborative relationships to call on for assistance. Unfortunately, your controlling, dominating, protectionist stance early on may have created more people happy to watch your demise rather than help you succeed. You will be isolated much like painting yourself into a corner.

Judgment is another powerful competitive anti-collaborative behavior. You often need support of partners and suppliers and other people in order for your business to deliver products reliably to your customers. Sometimes our desire to control these relationships too tightly prevents us from staying focused on the value to the customer. Instead, we become critical of insignificant aspects of these parties, and we focus an inordinate amount of time and energy on these minutiae.

How much more valuable would these relationship be if you could remain focused on your vision and your promise to customers, and devote energy with partners to aligning their focus in the same direction? The creativity and true value of what you can collectively deliver to your customers will increase dramatically. Now instead of judging minutiae you can judge productive outcomes as measured by your customers.

> You can't depend on your judgment when your imagination is out of focus.
>
> —Mark Twain

What would happen if we changed our attitude from a competitive mode to a cooperative mode?

CHAPTER 19:
Cooperation Accelerates Growth

For several years now, I have been concerned that my teenage son would not develop into a fully functioning adult man. From the age of about 14, he changed. I knew him to be an intelligent and articulate kid. Suddenly he appeared to become incapable of what I considered normal human communication. A series of grunts, monosyllables and shrugs of the shoulder seemed to be all he could muster. He would use this method to meet his basic needs of food, shelter and, of course, his game console and computer.

For the most part, this has been his mode of communication for a few years now. If you really want to hear him talk, ask him to tell you about his latest game. Not for us the easy and more familiar world of football scores or basketball plays. Our bonding moments these days occur over the tally of the number of kills he made, or the number of "golds" he earned, or the level in the game his latest character has attained. I have had to learn a new language in order to have a basic understanding of what occupies him for much of his time. To my anguish, he seemed destined for "super geek-dom". I could foresee him living a solitary life in front of a computer, tapping away at a virtual world, and disconnected from humankind. He would be conducting raids on foreign lands, killing, being killed, and then reviving himself at a keystroke to begin the game again.

Here's just a small peek into the new language I have learned: PVP (player versus player), RPG (role-playing games), raiding parties, FPS (first person shooter), MMOG (massively multiplayer online game), RTS (real time strategy), TBS (turn based strategy), NPC (non-player character), and perhaps appropriately for me (in spite of my age), "noob" (a newbie to the game world).

His mother, too, was concerned about his grades, future, socialization skills, and just how much he likes conquering others and killing his opponents. I reminded her that she sounded just like our grandparents did in the good old days. As kids, we did not mind our manners; we talked too much or not enough. Left to our own devices, we would run around outside pretending to be cops and robbers, killing each other. Then we would magically revive and "shoot" each other once again. Our weapons were fingers and sticks pointed at our targets, along with shouts of "POW!", and theatrical award-winning dying sequences.

A far cry from the virtual reality point and click world? Perhaps. It seems that the more things change, the more they stay the same. Without stereotyping or generalizing, "Boys will be boys," you may say. "It's our natural tendency to kill or be killed." "Survival of the fittest." "Dog eat dog." Game designers have tapped into this [psyche]. Take a look at some of the titles on my son's game library; "Warhammer", "Spore", "Star Wars" (hey, I recognize that one!), "World of Warcraft", "Dead Rising", "Gears of War", and "Grand Theft Auto", just to name a few. It is the way things are whether in corporate America, or on the inner city streets, or in countries torn by civil war. In so many ways, the games are in fact a reflection of the "real" world.

In these games that imitate life, the principle of competition and domination seems to be the rule. In order to win, whatever our circumstance may be, we set out to acquire and dominate all of the resources that will help us achieve our goals. Often times we ignore the impact these actions have on other people, and in fact, we even convince ourselves sometimes that the other people do not matter. They are competing for the same resource and therefore our goal is to eliminate them. Even if you succeed with this approach, you create two long-term problems for yourself. The first is that you make enemies out of everyone you encounter, including people on your own team. Their loyalty is very weak and secured only by fear. The second is that, even if you succeed at dominating a resource for a while, eventually all those competitors will find another way and your environment will change rapidly and not in a pleasant way. That will be the time when you need allies to help you evolve and to take on the next big opportunity. The problem is there will be nobody there to help you.

Players become proficient at raiding each other's worlds. They have trigger fingers that can hit that key so quickly you cannot even see the movement. Then when they play on-line with others, they get really smart about tactics. They learn to take orders from bosses, to collaborate with others, to complete their attacks successfully, and to wait their turn for rewards. The first time I heard that one, I wondered what happened to the old "That's just not fair" complaint, when measuring out how much soda he had compared with his older sister.

These days, my son comes out with an Australian expression that he learned from someone called Bruce. He might say something in Japanese that he heard last night, or he will say something about his friend in Holland. I have learned to expect all manner of strange words to come out of his mouth. However, when he speaks in a perfect Scottish accent, then I check under the bed to see if there is anything there that might explain this amazing transformation. The answer is that he's chatting to real people, real Aussies, Japanese or Dutch or Scotsmen. There is no age difference, self-consciousness, race, gender, shyness or embarrassment in his virtual world.

Everyone's on the same page, everyone has something in common. And—believe it or not—they are all talking to and cooperating with each other!

Being a concerned parent, I decided to do some research to see if I could understand his "condition". My mind was put somewhat at ease to find out that he was in the company of millions of others. The book by John C. Beck and Mitchell Wade titled "The Kids are Alright: How the Gamer Generation is Changing the Workplace" was a great help. If you have a teenage gamer or may be hiring young gamers, that book is a very helpful place to start.

Until now, success in his gaming world was a measure of body counts, size of territory and money in the bank. Gaming art imitating life in the real world (?). In business, we would all love to see the marketplace littered with the remains of our competitors. We would love to be "king" of our territory. And of course one of our major reasons for doing this is to put money in the bank. Exactly how do we do this? We do it by strategizing, by raiding, then attacking and eliminating our opponents, and ultimately reaping the rewards.

Even though my son learned a lot about collaborating and working with others in order to play these games successfully, the goal was always the same–domination. In business, we assemble large groups of people and partners to collaborate and cooperate with the same ultimate goal in mind. Some of those partners will attach themselves to a large company to ride the coat tails of its success. They hope to catch the breadcrumbs as it plunders its way through the market. All of the people involved seek the opportunity to make a "quick killing".

Dominate quickly, get rich, and get out. For every one that is successful, thousands of others find their business dried up. In this resource domination model, those without the means to acquire large numbers of resources quickly are simply not able to keep up. You might say "but this is the natural order of things in the competitive marketplace". You would be totally right. What we need to do is change the paradigm that we live in a competitive marketplace to one where cooperation is the rule. Cooperation enables us to take on much larger projects than we could ever dream of doing by ourselves by leveraging the strengths and resources of others.

Over dinner recently, my son was more quiet than usual. I knew that he had bought a new video game, which he had been playing for a few days. He said that the game had gone from super-easy and fun to ridiculously difficult. It had seemed so simple: "You get stuff and then you do stuff, and then you colonize space." He explained that you start by choosing the environment in which you would like to grow. You have a choice of forests, deserts, jungles, seashore, and so on. Then you decide whether you are a carnivore, herbivore, or omnivore. You get to choose personality traits like aggressive or collaborative.

Your character is now ready to be born. You have great flexibility in this area as well, being able to assemble creatures with the most unlikely features and limb structure. Of course, you need to make selections based on the environment you have chosen so that you can feed and move about successfully. Now you devour as much food as you can in your new domain and soon you stretch yourself beyond that to the world at large.

All the while, your character is growing in strength almost regardless of the characteristics you had chosen at the start. You are successfully becoming the leader of your world. You now go to the next level: outer space. Suddenly you face traveling to far away galaxies and meeting new strange creatures and conditions. All the tactics you learned from growing up in your home world no longer seem to work. My son's character was a very aggressive carnivore. He believed he needed to be the most powerful and awesome warrior he could be. He knew he would face many challenges. He was able to destroy and dominate anything that got in his way. By being the ultimate competitor, he became the conqueror of his world.

Once he got to outer space, however, he found many situations that he was not well equipped to manage. Food sources disappeared. As an aggressive character, he had an unusually large number of enemies and very few, if any, allies. It became clear to him very quickly that he had made a mistake. As a lone wolf aggressor, he was not going to survive. He needed the talents and skills of other characters, and he needed to be more versatile himself.

He found, by experience, that there is no way to win in this game, or any significant game, without learning how to cooperate with others. That means developing skills that are helpful to others, and matching other's skills to your unique needs at any given time. Without the right collaborative, team building, cooperative spirit, you will simply fade away.

In business, three key elements must align to create the potential for success. They are: 1. A compelling vision; 2. Comprehensive strategies to execute that vision; and 3. Committed leadership to achieve the vision and strategies. My son's experience shows us that leading with this spirit of cooperation will unleash the potential and catapult the business forward to the next level.

What a great lesson for a teenager. He learned that to execute your vision and strategies you need resources from others, including suppliers, operating systems, capital, and distribution. In a competitive model, your tendency is to protect your great ideas and your resources, and to exploit those provided by others. This wall of protection makes collaboration and the acquisition of resources very difficult, time-consuming, and expensive as everyone plays the same game.

The keystone of successful business is cooperation.
Friction retards progress.

—James Cash Penney

By adjusting your leadership attitude to one of cooperation, you effectively dissolve the wall and invite other people in. Suddenly you find people who are excited about your vision and want to help you make it happen. Others with specific resources or expertise can and will directly support the execution of your strategy. Acquiring motivated partners is easy and may cost you nothing as they all attach themselves to the bigger dream of your vision. Having many independent champions for your vision will expand your leadership beyond any limits you could imagine.

Cooperation makes the pie larger for everyone and it creates sustainable businesses built on the strength of a far more potent resource. What is that resource? In a word—"relationships". Cooperative relationships enable everyone to succeed, and they will be with you and you with them, when the next waves of change come along.

CONCLUSION

When we remove the protective walls, we find very quickly that some element of our business provides direct value to an element of another business. They, in turn, find the same is true for them. This accelerates the process of building and executing your business vision and strategy, and enables the cooperating parties to take on visions that are much bigger than they may ever have accomplished on their own. Each business recognizes that the overall pie can be much larger, and everyone has an opportunity to succeed. As more participants adopt this approach, the process accelerates faster.

The key influence at work in this model is that rather than target the scarcity of resources available to any one business, the focus becomes the relationships with other people and businesses. Those cooperative partnerships and alliances will not only play a big role in accelerating the business; they will create resilience for the business as market conditions evolve.

> A hundred times every day I remind myself that my inner and outer life depend on the labors of other men, living and dead, and that I must exert myself in order to give in the same measure as I have received and am still receiving.
>
> —Einstein, Albert

As brilliant a mathematician as he was, even Albert Einstein recognized the importance of his relationships with others and the importance of working hard to support and nurture them. Successful businesses in the future will most likely be those that learn to be the power of the waves of change with this cooperative attitude and integrate it within their businesses, as in the ebb and flow of tide.

Index

ABOUT THE AUTHOR

Patrick Smyth was born and raised in South Africa. He relocated to the US in 1981. He has served as a senior marketing and business executive with several Fortune 500 companies including AT&T, Tandem Computers, Compaq Computers, Ceridian, and WebMD/Emdeon. During that time, he developed, incubated, and re-branded several product businesses.

Patrick serves as a "business leadership navigator", working with CEOs and leaders of high growth businesses. Patrick is passionate about helping people be successful in their business endeavors. In his own words, "The power driving the next wave of change lives in the ideas and dreams of millions of entrepreneurs. Let's help them so they can help all of us."

He is a recognized speaker and author of the award-winning book Elephant Walk: Balancing Business Performance and Brand Strategy for the Long Haul. He has authored many articles on leadership and serves as a board level advisor to several businesses. Patrick is an instructor and mentor at CEO Space Forum where he trains and coaches thousands of business owners.

Patrick resides with his wife in a small town near Nashville TN. He enjoys gardening, puzzles, golf and bass fishing, when he has time.